In the Dry Desert

By Della Cohen

Scott Foresman
is an imprint of

PEARSON

Glenview, Illinois • Boston, Massachusetts • Chandler, Arizona •
Upper Saddle River, New Jersey

Photographs

Every effort has been made to secure permission and provide appropriate credit for photographic material. The publisher deeply regrets any omission and pledges to correct errors called to its attention in subsequent editions.

Unless otherwise acknowledged, all photographs are the property of Pearson Education, Inc.

Photo locators denoted as follows: Top (T), Center (C), Bottom (B), Left (L), Right (R), Background (Bkgd)

CVR Photolibrary; **1** © Jim Parkin /Alamy Images; **3** Photolibrary; **4** © Jim Parkin /Alamy Images; **5** © Robert Shantz/Alamy Images; **6** ©Design Pics Inc/Alamy; **7** John Cancalosi/ SuperStock; **8** ©image100/SuperStock

ISBN 13: 978-0-328-46334-3
ISBN 10:   0-328-46334-5

1 2 3 4 5 6 7 8 9 10 V0G1 13 12 11 10 09

I see a cactus.

I see a flower.

I see a prairie dog.

I see a lizard.

I see a hawk.

I see rain!